Heaton, Byker & Walker
In Old Picture Postcards

by Andrew Clark & George Nairn

A postcard of children in Sunningdale Avenue, Walker, from the early 1900s. It has this message on the back: 'What do you think of our house third on the right side?'

Previous page: A party in Quality Row, Byker to celebrate the end of the First World War. Many are in fancy dress, including on the far right the iconic 'Charlie Chaplin'.

Acknowledgements

The authors would like to thank the following who have helped with the publication of this book: Alan Brett, Philip Curtis, Tommy Finn, Edward Simpson, Sharyn Taylor, Yvonne Young, Beamish – The North of England Open Air Museum.

Bibliography

Bygone High Heaton by William Muir, Newcastle City Library and Arts, 1988
Bygone Walker by Liz Michael, Newcastle City Library and Arts, 1992
Heaton – from farms to foundries by Alan Morgan, Tyne Bridge Publishing, 2012
Monthly Chronicle of North Country Lore and Legend, 1888
Old Ordnance Survey Maps – Walker & Hebburn, 1895 by Alan Godfrey

The Evening Chronicle; The Journal; The Shipyard Magazine

Introduction

Heaton, Byker and Walker are popular areas of Newcastle to live, work and play. For a number of years I lived in Heaton and worked in schools and youth centres in Byker and Walker. I also spent happy days in Heaton and Armstrong Parks; nights at the People's Theatre; or many shopping trips along Shields Road. In my time in this part of Newcastle I met many people who were proud of their community and its history.

The area has seen many changes and some of these changes are featured in the photographs in this book. The majority of the illustrations are taken from old picture postcards that show the streets, schools, churches, shops, factories, railway stations and pubs of Heaton, Byker and Walker. People are also featured – from sewing groups to football teams. As well as postcards, there are also drawings, adverts and some more modern photographs, including a few 'then and now' comparisons showing how streets have changed over the past 100 years.

Andrew Clark
Summerhill Books, 2013

A picture postcard view of Simonside Terrace, Heaton from before the First World War.

Picture Postcards

The golden age of the picture postcard was from the beginning of the twentieth century to the First World War. Therefore many of the images in this book show Heaton, Byker and Walker around one hundred years ago.

Now, we rarely send a postcard unless perhaps on holiday. A century ago, posting a card was as common as sending a text or email. On the back of the postcards are often very simple messages such as 'How are you?' or 'Will see you soon' – the sort of things we would put into a text today. We have included some of the messages that were on the back of the cards alongside their images.

Messages often refer to the photographs on the front of the postcard – pointing out where people live, work or go to school. Sending cards like these to friends was similar to posting photographs on Facebook or other social networks today.

The area was popular for postcard photographers such as Robert Johnston of Gateshead who came to Walker one day in the 1920s to take pictures of the Stack Hotel, the Mechanics' Institute and Welbeck Road – all featured in this book. These photographs now provide a vivid, historic record that can be enjoyed by local people in search of their heritage.

3

Old Heaton, Byker & Walker

The ruins known as King John's Palace in Heaton Park. There is no direct connection with King John and the building is believed to have been a fortified house belonging to Adam of Jesmond, dating back to the thirteenth century. It is now a lovely landmark in the redeveloped park.

King John's Well in Armstrong Park. An old stone trough was found near King John's Palace when the park was being developed in the 1880s and was moved to the site of a spring. The inscription – 'Ye Well of King John' was added at that time.

Left: Heaton Hall – home of the wealthy Ridley family from the early 1700s to mid 1840s. The Hall was then occupied by the Potter family till shortly before it was demolished in 1933. Housing was then built on the site of the hall and grounds, just off Heaton Road.

The former Byker residence of the Lawson family in the eighteenth century.

The Old Manor House at Byker in the eighteenth century.

The coal mining traditions of the area were immortalised in the song *Byker Hill*. Written in the 1800s, the song is still popular today and performed by local bands such as the 'Whiskey Priests' and 'Kiddar's Luck'.

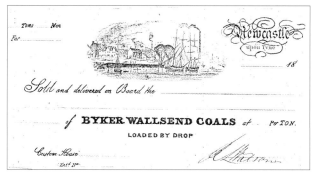

A loading note for 'Byker Wallsend Coals'.

Right: A nineteenth century coal hewer in a Tyneside pit. The men had to endure poor pay, harsh working conditions and very little health and safety.

BYKER HILL

If I had another penny
I would have another gill
I would make the piper play
The 'Bonny Lass o' Byker Hill'

Chorus
Byker Hill and Walker Shore
Collier lads for ever more!
Byker Hill and Walker Shore
Collier lads for ever more!

When first I came down to the dirt
I had no coat and no pit shirt
Now I've gotten two or three
Walker Pit's done well by me

The pitman and the keelman trim
They drink bumble made from gin
Then to dance they do begin
To the tune of 'Elsie Marley'.

The poor coalcutter gets a shilling
The deputy get half a crown
The overman gets five and six
Just for riding up and down

Geordie Charlton had a pig
He hit it with a shovel and it danced a jig
All the way to Walker Shore
To the tune of 'Elsie Marley'.

Walker Quay, around 1830 – an illustration by J.W. Carmichael.

Glimpses of Heaton

Left: Heaton Road looking towards Shields Road before the First World War. On the right is the Cuthbert Bainbridge Memorial Methodist Chapel, named after a member of the department store family. On the left is the Congregational Church.

Left: Heaton Road in 2013. The Cuthbert Bainbridge Memorial Methodist Chapel has gone but the Congregational Church remains – now called the Elim Pentecostal Church. In the distance is the distinctive building of the Lloyds Bank on Shields Road.

Right: The sewing circle of Cuthbert Bainbridge Memorial Methodist Chapel around 1890. The church has been demolished and replaced with the Ark – a youth and community centre.

Left: Heaton Road looking towards Shields Road around 1905. The grand looking house on the far left has today been replaced by a modern office block. Note, in the middle of the road, the ornate tram line posts.

Right: Heaton Road, around 1908. On the left is the Presbyterian Church with the church hall just further along on the corner of Cardigan Terrace. Plenty of shops on this part of Heaton Road with the Co-op buildings on the left past the church.

Right: Heaton Road in 2013. Still a busy part of Heaton Road with cars replacing the cycles and horse and cart of the postcard above. The Presbyterian Church has now gone and replaced with flats, although the church hall remains.

Left: A postcard view of Heaton Road, around 1905. This was originally a coloured postcard and the photograph was taken from the corner of Cardigan Terrace. The Co-op buildings can just be seen to the far left. In the distance are the grounds of Heaton Hall, now the site of housing.

Left: Heaton Road in 2013. Now a busy junction with traffic lights. The building on the left is no longer the Co-op and has been divided up into a number of other shops and businesses. However, the building still has the sign 'Newcastle-upon-Tyne Co-operative Society Limited 1892.'

Heaton Baptist Church, Heaton Road. A postcard published by H. Denholm Brash, Bookseller and Stationer of Newcastle.

The Midland Bank, 112 Heaton Road in the 1920s. Kelly's trade directory of 1929 records that T.H. Pugh was the manager and the telephone number was 'City 54'. Is that Mr Pugh in the centre of the three men? This was a time of a more personal service from you local bank and your business was discussed face to face with the manager or his staff – not through a telephone call centre like today. The building is now an lettings agency.

More personal service in this photograph of Robinson's Pork Shop at 74 Heaton Road. Plenty of customers in this busy shop around 1970. In 2013 the shop still sells food but is now an Indian takeaway.

Heaton is known for its many streets of terraced housing, particularly just off Heaton Road and Chillingham Road. Here are some postcard views of local streets.

Above: Simonside Terrace. The sender of this postcard has written on the back: 'This is a view of our terrace, it looks nice on a postcard but it really is a nice street. It is very quiet being at the outskirts of the city.'

Left: Cartington Terrace around 1905.

Two views of Rothbury Terrace. On the left a scene from around 1905. On the right a couple of lads on bikes are the only ones in the road. Today, streets like this are packed with parked cars.

Above: Heaton Park Road, around 1910. A postcard sent to County Durham, the message on the back says: 'How do you like this card. My home is at the corner near the park gates.'

Right: Heaton Park Entrance, around 1904. On the right is Garden Cottage.

Two quiet streets just off Heaton Park View before the First World War. *Left*: Children in Holmside Place. *Right*: Kingsley Place with the Victoria Library in the distance. Built to commemorate Queen Victoria's 1897 Diamond Jubilee, the library was open for over a century. Today, the building is home to apartments and business premises.

Right: St Gabriel's Parish Hall on the corner of Chillingham Road and Cartington Terrace. The hall was opened in 1925 and this spacious building was used for many years by a number of groups in the parish. It is now home to St Gabriel's Children Day Nursery.

Left: The interior of Chillingham Road Council School, around 1905. On the back is a touching message from one of the children at the school: 'Dear Grandpa. How are you getting on. When are you coming to see us again. I hope you are all well. This is the large room where we all drill.'

Heaton United AFC, 1909-10. The goalkeeper is holding an old case ball that soaked up water in the wet while the players have the old style boots – very different from today's kit. How many of these lads were involved in the horrors of the First World War, only a few years away?

Above: A.S. Wilkin Ltd's Cremona Toffee Works, Cremona Park in 1938. The factory on Benton Road is now the site of a supermarket and car dealership. In the years before and after the Second World War it was common to have a sweet, toffee or pop factory in the community. A.S. Wilkin were said to be a good employer that looked after their workers and provided good conditions in their factories. To the right is the Byker and Heaton Cemetery.

Right: An advert for Charleton's Dairy, 15 Cornel Road, High Heaton. This dairy provided regular deliveries within a ten mile radius and the milk was 'tuberculin tested'.

Telephone: Newcastle 661685 and 661219

Charleton's Dairy

Proprietor: B. Charleton

Jersey . Tuberculin Tested
Pasteurised Milk   Orange Juice
Fresh Cream
Regular deliveries within a ten mile radius

15 Cornel Road

High Heaton

Girls getting on a bus after finishing their day at Heaton Secondary Schools. For many years the school was split into Heaton High School for Girls on Newton Road (seen here) while on the other side of the site was Heaton Grammar School for Boys. In 1983 the school merged with Manor Park on Benton Road and became known as Heaton Manor School. In 2003 to 2004, a new school was built on Newton Road and the Benton Road site was demolished for house-building

The King and Queen in Heaton

King George V and Queen Mary at Heaton Secondary Schools on 10th October 1928.

The *Evening Chronicle* on that day reported: 'Soon after nine the long procession of school children made their way towards Heaton Secondary Schools, where they were to greet their Majesties. Thousands came by train from all parts of the city. It was a great day for them as was seen from the bright, expectant look on so many thousands of young faces. From eighty schools they came, nearly 24,000 of them shepherded by teachers who seemed as eager over the event as the children themselves. The spacious play grounds by careful allotment of space, found room for all. At 9.45 the privileged spectators were admitted, and as a result of the excellence of the arrangements that had been made there was nothing in the way of undue hurry. As the hour of the Royal arrival drew near the great multitude of children grew happily excited. They had come to cheer and in the waiting period they found much which they could cheer … There were further lusty, shrill cheers and waving of thousands of handkerchiefs as a welcome for the city's representatives. Then, a few minutes before it was expected, came the great moment. Cheers were redoubled, echoing through the quadrangles, rising shrill through the clear autumn air. The King and Queen had come.'

Left: A postcard view of Heaton Secondary Schools shortly after it was built in 1928.

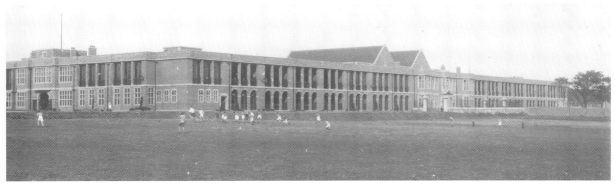

A football match at the Heaton Secondary Schools. The school was officially opened by George V on his visit in 1928.

The King gave this speech at the school: 'I am happy to receive your loyal and dutiful address and the Queen and I are deeply touched by the affectionate welcome accorded to us by the citizens of Newcastle upon Tyne. It is a great pleasure to us to have this opportunity to see so vast an assembly of school children, and of visiting the new Heaton Secondary School. I congratulate the Education Authority of the city upon the provision of these finely-constructed and well equipped buildings which, I am confident will mark a great step in advance for secondary education in Newcastle.

'The primary object of today's visit, the opening of the Tyne Bridge, recalls a like occasion in the past that forms another association of my family with your city for in 1906 my dear father came here to open the bridge which bears his name.

'It is a source of much grief to me to know that during the past few years the men and women in this area have been living under the shadow of grave industrial depression. Owing to the dislocation of trade caused by the War, the industries of coal, iron and steel and shipbuilding, which have given worldwide renown to the River Tyne, have been struggling with adversity.

'The erection of the New Bridge is a characteristic act of courage, and demonstrates your belief in the power of these industries to recover lost trade and to play again their former proud role in the world's market.

'I am happy to observe that your dauntless handling of these difficulties achieving results. Already the coal industry of the North and the shipbuilding of the Tyne appear to be emerging from the depression. I trust that this day may be the beginning of a new era of prosperity and that God's Blessing may ever rest upon your city.'

After leaving Heaton, the King and Queen officially opened the newly built Tyne Bridge.

The construction of the bridge in January 1928. By October of that year, building work was finished!

Glimpses of Byker

OUSEBURN, NEWCASTLE.

Left: A picturesque illustration of the viaduct over the Ouseburn. Built in 1839 with some re-structuring since, the viaduct now carries the East Coast Main Line. Byker Bridge (*below*) was built in 1878 and until 1895 a halfpenny toll was charged to cross. The bridge has seen a number of improvements; most recently in the mid 1980s.

Right: Byker Bridge around 1911. A busy scene with carts, pedestrians and trams in the distance. This was a postcard sent to France and the message on the back says: 'This is the bridge I cross to go to Newcastle. It is nice and wide … After I have sent this card I am going out to the shops.'

BYKER BRIDGE, NEWCASTLE.

Dear Ethel. One more card, for your collection, from Alice.

Left: A closer view of the bridge – a postcard sent in 1905. On the front is the message: 'Dear Ethel, one more card, for your collection, from Alice.' A hundred years after this was sent, collecting postcards is still a popular hobby.

Above: The Grand Theatre on Wilfred Street was built in the 1890s and during its working life showed both films and plays. The theatre survived into the 1950s before closing and the building was demolished the following decade.

Top right: An advertising card for the play 'In Holy Russia' featuring Mrs J. Cassidy at the Grand Theatre on 23rd November 1908.

Right: Adverts for two local cinemas from the 1950s. The Lyric, Heaton was showing a Dean Martin and Jerry Lewis film. While the Apollo, Byker had *The Baby & the Battleship* with John Mills and Richard Attenborough.

Above: An ice cream stand belonging to Risi's Ices of Byker. Unfortunately, it is not known where this photograph was taken – perhaps the Hoppings on the Town Moor?

Right: An advert for Risi's Ices from 1929. They had their factory and offices on Wilfred Street and a branch on Shields Road. They had previously had premises on Byker Bank. Risi's supplied hotels, restaurants and theatres – including the Theatre Royal in Newcastle.

The two images on the left are from coloured postcards produced by F. Beavan Ltd to advertise their products. They show one of Frederick Beavan's earliest shops in the early 1900s.

Both cards have printed on the reverse: 'Dear Madam. Our celebrated series of private Christmas Cards for the 1907-08, including the best designs by leading makers, are now ready. Prices from 1s per dozen. On receipt of postcard, we shall be pleased to send samples for inspection. F. Beavan Ltd.'

Right: Beavan's later store on Shields Road in 2013. A number of shops and other businesses have occupied the building since Beavan's closed, although the store's name and its advertising for – 'Ironmongers' and 'Furnishers' remain on view.

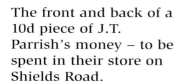

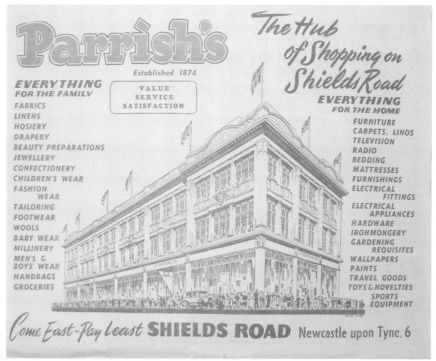

The front and back of a 10d piece of J.T. Parrish's money – to be spent in their store on Shields Road.

An advert for Parrish's from 1953. The advert boasts: 'Come East – Pay Least'. People would travel from well outside the area to do their shopping at Parrish's with its many departments. The building is now student accommodation with retail units on the ground floor.

Above: A cake made of butter to promote the Meadow Dairy.

Right: Meadow Dairy, 106 Shields Road. James Ryan, one of seven staff, is in the centre of the group in the doorway.

A tram trundles down Shields Road, around 1910. Some of the shops on the left include: Gilbert Foggin fishmonger, R. Forster's cafe, D. Young furniture broker and J. Teago cash draper.

The Byker Branch of Barclays Bank, 102-104 Shields Road. In 1929 the manager of the bank was Mr R. Stewart. A new branch of Barclays is now on this part of Shields Road.

An advert from 1953 for Pledger's Drapers & Furnishers, 212-216 Shields Road. Herbert Pledger & Co also had premises at number 220 Shields Road. The building above now houses Nobles Amusements.

Inside Anderson's Jewellers at 90-92 Shields Road around the 1960s. In the glass display cases are, amongst other items, watches, tankards and hip flasks.

R.A. Dodds Meat Contractor of 237 Shields Road, around 1930. The butchers seem to be proud of their display of meat in the window. In 2013 the shop is now occupied by Cardarama – greeting cards, fancy goods and stationery.

Left: Two photographs of celebrations in Byker. The top picture shows the residents of Headlam Street, possibly in the 1930s while celebrating George V's Jubilee or the coronation of George VI. Unfortunately, the location and occasion of the bottom picture is unknown. Perhaps it is a church parade. The photograph was taken by Will Arnold, 14 Solway Street, Byker.

Men, dogs and boy in Quality Row, Byker, around 1900.

The Raby Hotel on Shields Road between the two world wars. The pub is still serving customers today and Shields Road continues to be a popular area for drinkers with a number of establishments surviving the down turn in trade of recent years. The pub has had some renovations over the years but the ornate metalwork around the windows seen here has survived to 2013.

Left: An advert for Ringtons Tea from 1957. It features the slogan 'free deliveries to all parts by own vans' and shows the well known Ringtons building in Algernon Road. The business was started by William Titterington and Samuel Smith in 1907. Later Smith bought out his partner. The Algernon Road factory was purpose-built in 1926 and remained in operation until 1992 when a new factory was opened at Longbenton. The old premises was taken over by the auctioneers Thomas N. Miller (*seen above in 2013*). However, Ringtons still use a building nearby.

Right: Two Byker buses – an early single decker and a later double decker. *Below*: A Byker tram. The much loved tram system started in Newcastle in 1901 and lasted for almost 50 years. There was a tram depot in Byker as well as Wingrove in the west and Haymarket in the city centre. By the 1920s there were 300 trams running in Newcastle.

Right: James Melville's Bakery, 92 Raby Street, around 1935. Standing in the doorway are: Cissy Anderson, Thomas Melville (son of the owner) and Mary Melville (sister of the owner). Wedding and birthday cakes are advertised in the window as well as Turog bread.

Left: Raby Street in the 1970s during a time of redevelopment in the area. Three ladies look in the window of J.J. Glendinning and Son outfitters. A woman dressed in fashionable flared trousers poses for the camera. Next door is a pawnbroker's shop. On the far left are the three golden balls – the sign of a pawnbroker – a shop used by many when times were hard.

The late 1960s and '70s were to see Byker transformed with the demolition of hundreds of houses and the construction of the 'Wall' development. In the early 1970s Newcastle Council produced a booklet to promote the new development and it included a section on 'The Corner Shops':

'The corner shop plays a very important part in Byker and special provision will be made for new ones. The plan shows a large number of suitable locations, although it is unlikely that all these will be taken up. Raby Street is planned to remain as a hub of activity and there is likely to be a grouping of shops on Raby Street north of Commercial Road, where a site for a new public house is also being provided.'

Left: St Mark's Church and Parish Hall on Shields Road. The church was consecrated in 1906. Now no longer a place of worship, today the building is the home of the Newcastle Climbing Centre. Many local churches have been closed and demolished so it is good that this building is still in use by the community

Right: A First World War postcard sent from St Mark's Church, Byker Hill – as the area was then known. The message was for sailors at Christmastide and the original card is printed in colour – the rainbow standing out amongst the dark clouds. Millions of postcards were sent to servicemen during the war.

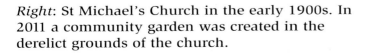

Above: The interior of St Michael's Church, Byker. The church was built in 1862.

Right: St Michael's Church in the early 1900s. In 2011 a community garden was created in the derelict grounds of the church.

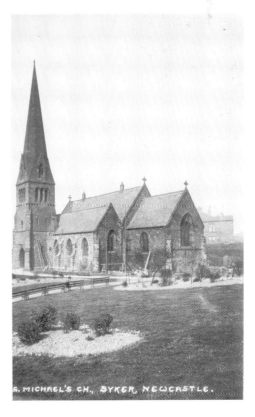

Glimpses of Walker

Left: Walker Police Station on the corner of Wharrier Street and Rochester Street. This postcard was titled 'The New Police Station' so will date from shortly after it was opened in 1908. This wonderful looking building was to serve the area for 60 years.

Left: The demolition of Walker Police Station in 1970. The block of flats behind the station are now gone themselves and new houses have been built on the site. This is a common story of the changing face of Walker.

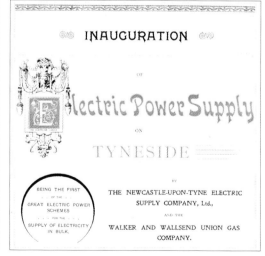

INAUGURATION

OF

Electric Power Supply

ON

TYNESIDE

BY

THE NEWCASTLE-UPON-TYNE ELECTRIC
SUPPLY COMPANY, Ltd.,

AND THE

WALKER AND WALLSEND UNION GAS
COMPANY.

BEING THE FIRST
OF THE
GREAT ELECTRIC POWER
SCHEMES
FOR THE
SUPPLY OF ELECTRICITY
IN BULK.

Above left: Pipelayers of the Walker and Wallsend Union Gas Company, 6th April 1904.
Above right: The title page from a booklet published to celebrate the opening of the Neptune Bank Power Station on 18th June 1901. The station was built by the Newcastle-upon-Tyne Electric Supply Company and the Walker and Wallsend Union Gas Company. Lord Kelvin was guest of honour at the official opening and following the inauguration, a luncheon was held at the Drill Hall in Walker.

...WCASTLE FLOODS, SEP, 1913.
19. WALKER GATE.

A postcard showing flash floods in Walker Gate in September 1913. This area has frequently suffered from flooding including on 28th June 2012 – the night the Tyne Bridge was struck with lightning. In September 1913 the *Journal* newspaper reported: 'The spell of dry weather in the north was broken on Saturday, when during the early morning a severe thunderstorm was experienced in Newcastle and district, accompanied by a heavy rainfall shortly after five o'clock lightening flashed vividly and was followed by loud peals of thunder. At this time the rain descended in torrents.'

The article went on to describe the storm damage in Pegswood, Northumberland: 'The thunderstorm of Saturday morning proved of exceptional severity at Pegswood Colliery. Robert Allison, 302 Welbeck Terrace, was struck by lightning, and fell in an unconscious state on the floor. He is under medical attendance, and is slowly recovering. Thomas Fox, 357 Bolsover Terrace, was filling the poss tub from the water barrel, when there was a vivid flash of lighting. He was dazed, but managed to get into the house, where he collapsed and became paralysed. He is also under medical treatment, and is slowly recovering, but is still confined to bed. The atmosphere was so surcharged with electricity that many children and grown-up persons fainted.'

Right: Walker Celtic FC in 1935-36 season. Back row: W. Brown (trainer), G. Lewins, J. Simpson, J. Scott, R. Wood, S. Graham, W. Cotterell. Front row: J. Ferguson, W. Easton (captain), J. West, F. McKenna, T. Crooks. This is one of dozens of North East football teams featured on Ardath Tobacco cigarette cards. On the back of this card is the following information on the club: 'Have won many league championships. In 1927-28 were transferred to the 2nd

WALKER CELTIC F.C.

Division of the North Eastern League, and in 1929-30 promoted to the 1st Division. In 1934-35 and 1935-36 the club received runners-up medals for non-reserve teams.'

Left: Welbeck Road in the 1970s with the post office, J.K. Bingham's newsagents, Ladbrokes and Welbeck Fruiterers. The post office and Bingham's are still trading today. Welbeck Fruiterers is now the Welbeck Road Pet Store.

Left: The interior of Bingham's in the 1970s. Note the old scales to weigh bags of sweets out of the jar. Also the box on the counter for 'cross the ball'. Competitions like the football pools and 'spot the ball' were very popular in the days before the Lottery.

Welbeck Road in the early 1900s. Another post office, this time Byker Street Post Office, is in the centre.

Right: A postcard of Welbeck Road from the early 1920s. This image was taken by the excellent postcard photographer Robert Johnston. On the left is a branch of the grocers Walter Willson's.

Welbeck Road, Walker.

Right: A view of Welbeck Road in 2013. The Walter Willson's has gone and now replaced by a modern convenience store. The tram lines have also disappeared and modern road traffic requires a set of lights.

Left: A closer view of Walter Willson's on Welbeck Road. The company advertised that they were the 'smiling service shop' and took great pride in their window displays.

Left: Welbeck Road in the early 1920s. The house on the far right has the following inscription: 'Queen Victoria Memorial. This residence was presented to the Walker Nursing Association by Henry F. Swan Esq CB and Mrs Swan, 1902'. At the time this photo was taken, the matron of the Nursing Association was Miss Francis Brotherton.

Left: Welbeck Road in 2013. The church in the picture above has now gone and trees and a block of flats are in its place.

Children crowd around a tram on Welbeck Road in the early 1900s.

Right: Two men take a break from building a rail bridge over Welbeck Road to pose for the cameraman. The bridge was for the riverside branch railway line. The line opened in May 1879 between Manors and Percy Main with passenger services ceasing in July 1973. This line was not converted to the Metro system, though it would have helped with urban congestion.

A postcard of Christ Church – Walker Parish Church. Built in 1848, funding of the church came from the owners of the shipyards and engineering firms in the area.

The interior of Walker Parish Church.

The Monument of Robert 'Honest Bob' Chambers in Walker Churchyard. Chambers was born in St Anthony's in 1831 and became a professional oarsman. He won the Tyne, Thames, English and World Sculling Championships. Sadly, he died when only 37 years old and was buried in Walker. His ill health was thought to be from working in a local iron foundry in his youth.

Mechanics Institute, Walker. 3597

WALKER CO-OPERATIVE SOCIETY LTD

Above: A postcard titled 'Mechanics Institute, Walker'. The card, produced by Johnston of Gateshead, was posted in 1925. To the right is the Presbyterian Church.

Left: A branch of the Walker Co-operative Society. Kelly's Trade Directory of 1929 lists branches of the Walker Co-op at 1 Lamb Street, 561 Welbeck Road, 77 Church Street and 868 & 900 Shields Road, Walker Gate.

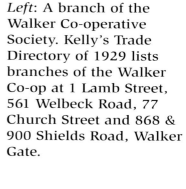

Left: A Walker Co-op delivery cart. The Co-op offered home deliveries as well as the all-important 'divi' paid to customers who gave their number when purchasing goods. Many people today still remember their Co-op dividend numbers.

Left: Pottery Bank, St Anthony's. At the time this photograph was taken in the early 1900s, four shopkeepers were listed in trade directories to have lived here as well as a grocer, riveter and coal merchant. This area was demolished during slum clearances in the 1930s.

Right: Walker Road, St Anthony's – a postcard sent to a Mrs Pickering of Church Street, Walker-on-Tyne in 1922. The message says: 'Dear Mrs P. I'm sending you this just to refresh your memory of the old place. Places of interest of course – butchers, fish shop, store and the school. Hope you better. Kind regards Bella.'

St Anthony of Padua Girls and Infants School. Note the roof surrounded by railings – this would be where the children would go outside and play

Model Cottage Exhibition at Walker

Right: The Lord Mayor of Newcastle opens the North of England Model Cottage Exhibition at Walker on 23rd June 1908.

The *Journal* at the time gave this description of the Exhibition:

'For many years, the housing problem in our large centre of population has occupied the attention of social reformers and the promoters of this exhibition have endeavoured to put into practical operation some, at any rate, of the more national ideas which have been formulated on the subject.

'Sixteen and a half acres on the Walker estate of the City Corporation were handed over to the committee (of the Exhibition) for the purpose of showing what could be done in putting their ideas into practice. The object of the venture were agreed upon as follows: (1) To promote examples of model suburb planning under existing bye-laws; (2) to estimate the building of well designed comfortable homes capable of being within the means of workmen; and (3) to provide architects and builders desirous of improving upon existing methods of building and planning workmen's cottages, with the opportunity of showing the value of their improvements in a definite and practical way. In order to carry out their objects the committee first held a competition for architects as to the best planning out of the land so far as streets and general estate arrangements were concerned after which builders and architects were invited to display their skills in the designing and creation of three classes of cottages.

'Class A contains two bedrooms, a large living room and scullery, the maximum price to be £195. Class B contains three bedrooms, a large living room and scullery, the maximum price being £235. Class C contains three bedrooms, parlour, large living room and scullery, the maximum price to be £260. One of the conditions was a bath must be provided in each house. The price does not of course include the cost of land or ordinary estate charges, such as road making, proportional costs of sewer etc but embraces architects' charge and building profits. The land is leasehold and may be secured from the Corporation at a fixed rental. Before building operations were commenced it was suggested that other classes might be added. Consequently the additional types were included – Class D cottage with the number of rooms not specified, the maximum price £350 and a special class suitable for newly married couples to contain bed and living rooms and scullery, the price not to exceed £150.'

The entrance to the Model Cottage Exhibition.

Right:
Briarwood
Crescent,
Walkerville,
around 1912 –
one of the
streets built for
the North of
England Model
Cottage
Exhibition –
affordable and
comfortable
homes for local
families.

Right:
Briarwood
Crescent in
2013. These
houses, just off
Shields Road,
are still a great
example of
family homes a
century after
they were built.

Left:
Walkerville
Post Office run
by Guilfoyle
Grocers. In
Kelly's Trade
Directory of
1929, a Mr
Peter Guilfoyle
is listed as a
grocer at
Number 1002,
Shields Road.

Neptune Works During the First World War

Women workers in the Shell Shop of the Neptune Works, Walker, of Swan, Hunter & Wigham Richardson during the First World War.

The *Shipyard Magazine* of February 1919 published the following article about a party for those who had worked in the Shell Shop during the war:

On Saturday, 7th December 1918, there took place a most interesting function in the Heaton Assembly Rooms, in connection with the firm of Messrs Swan, Hunter & Wigham Richardson Ltd. The work in the Shell Shop of the firm having come to an end, by the termination of hostilities, a farewell party was kindly given by the Directors and Management of the Neptune Works to the girls and men who for the last three years have laboured to turn out ammunition for our forces abroad.

The invitations were from 3 to 6.30, and after a sumptuous tea, to which everyone did full justice, an adjournment was made to the ballroom, where the most interesting ceremony of the afternoon took place. The chair was taken by G. Vardy Esq, and on the platform were Lady Hunter, Mr and Mrs G.F. Tweedy, Captain J.H. Bruce (Engineer and Secretary of the local Board of Management of the Ministry of Munitions) and Mrs Bruce, Captain Thorne, Mr and Mrs Yates, Miss Harvey, Mr and Mrs Morgan and others.

The Chairman first expressed the regrets of Sir G.B. Hunter and Mr and Mrs Denham Christie, who were unable to be present. After welcoming guests, he said that they were met together on this auspicious occasion to say farewell, after being closely associated for almost the whole period of the War. He wished to take the opportunity, on behalf of the workers – the girls and women particularly – for the excellent work they had done during that long time. He emphasised the appreciation of the Directors and Management at the good feeling and *esprit de corps* that had always existed in the Shell Shop.

In conclusion, he had the pleasant duty to perform, to call upon Mrs Tweddy to present mementoes to seven of the women workers whose names had been chosen from the records kept of their work; also to six women workers who had been in the Shell Shop from the commencement. The presents, which consisted of gold bracelets (with inscriptions) for the first seven and gold bar brooches for the second number (whose names were chosen by the firm), were kindly given by G.F. Tweddy, Esq, one of the Directors. Mrs Tweddy then made the presentations amidst much applause.

Mr Tweddy, responding on Mrs Tweddy's behalf, said how pleased he was to have the opportunity of meeting them all once more. Their labours had come to an end, and it would no doubt be a source of gratification to them all to remember in the years to come that their individual efforts had helped to win the war. He wished them all 'good luck'. He had heard that many of the girls had lost their war badges, and he hoped that when they received permission from the Minister of Munitions to retain their war badges they would all be able to remember the different places wherein they had mislaid them. (Loud applause.)

Mr Yates, manager of the Shell Shop, then spoke, giving a brief resume of the work done since the commencement of the shop, and then proposed a hearty vote of thanks to Mr and Mrs Tweddy for their kindness and generosity, which was seconded by Miss Nicholson and carried with acclamation. The remainder of the afternoon was passed in dancing interspersed with songs.

Two interesting presentations took place on the evening of 23rd December 1918, at the Neptune Works, when Miss Harvey, the chief Welfare Supervisor, and Mrs Quinn, the Shipyard Forewoman, were the recipients of very handsome presents from the girls employed in the Shipyard Department.

The donors had taken this opportunity for their presentation, as they all felt that the time was shortly coming when they would be asked to give up their work to the returning soldiers, and they might not be able to all meet together again. Miss Harvey received a silver and tortoise shell inlaid box and Mrs Quinn a silver-plated tea service.

The presentations were made in the girls' messroom, which had been gaily decorated for the occasion, and later an excellent tea was served. The rest of the evening was spent in dancing.

The letterhead of the Neptune Works, Walker, of Swan, Hunter & Wigham Richardson from the First World War.

Left: The football team and officials of the Neptune Engine Works, Walker, 1917-18. Although the war was on at the time, there was still time for football for these lads.

CA Parsons

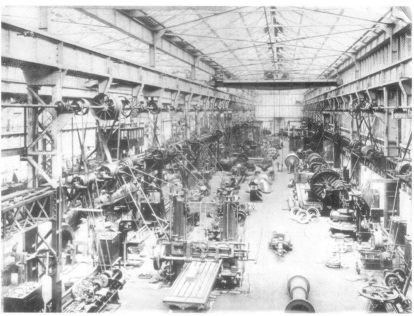

Charles A. Parsons, who started his engineering works in Heaton in 1889, became a world leader in the manufacture of turbines and electrical equipment.

The interior of CA Parsons' Works on Shields Road, Heaton. The most famous of the many inventions and innovations of Parsons was the *Turbinia* – the first vessel in the world to be powered by a turbine. Built in 1894, the *Turbinia* now has pride of place near the entrance of the Discovery Museum in Newcastle.

Left: A new Ferrybridge rotor being hauled by a Hunslet diesel shunter in February 1963. A cold working environment for these men with snow on the ground.

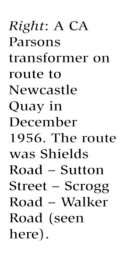

Right: A CA Parsons transformer on route to Newcastle Quay in December 1956. The route was Shields Road – Sutton Street – Scrogg Road – Walker Road (seen here).

A crane girder being transported through CA Parsons on 8th March 1963. At the top centre can be seen the cabin for controlling the internal railway system.

The crane girder crossing Shields Road on 8th March 1963, causing some traffic hold ups.

Right: A telescope section being loaded on to a trailer at Grubb Parsons, Shields Road. The company was world renowned for its manufacturing of telescopes with the Royal Observatory being one of its customers. The Grubb Telescope Company was founded in Dublin in 1833 and produced optical instruments for nearly a century before being acquired by Sir Charles Parsons in 1925.

A Drax Outer Casing going up Byker Bank from Hawthorn Leslie to CA Parsons. It is being hauled by two Pickford Scamell Tractors.

Public Houses

Stack Hotel, Church Street, Walker. 3596

Above: The Stack Hotel, Church Street, Walker in the early 1920s. This pub was demolished during one of the many redevelopments of the area.

Left: Men in fancy dress outside the Stack Hotel raising money for the Walker Distress Fund for children. Local groups such as this were often formed during hard times such as strikes or accidents at mines or factories.

The Scrogg Inn, Walker in 1963. While many pubs in the area have closed and even been demolished, this pub is still open in 2013 and the exterior has hardly changed.

Walker Gate.

The Wolsington Hotel in Walker Gate from an Auty of Tynemouth postcard dated around 1900. Outside the pub are a number of horse and carts as well as a tram that looks like the top deck is full with passengers.

The Royal Oak, Walker Road, 1953.

The Heaton Hotel, Shields Road, in 1963.

Two views of the Tanners Arms on the approach to Byker Bridge. On the left a view from between the World Wars while on the right the same scene in 2013. A policeman stands directing traffic where today there is a set of lights.

'Heaton for Byker'

Left: A very early view of Heaton Railway Station in the late 1800s, possible shortly after building work in 1887. The station offices and waiting room were built over the railway tracks – as seen in the photograph at the bottom of the page. Note the sign 'Heaton for Byker'.

Left: A view of the two platforms of the station that was on Heaton Road. As in the postcard above, staff and passengers pose for the photographer – showing off their new station perhaps?

Below: Heaton Railway Station in its later years. The station was closed in 1980 and demolished.

Walker Park

A postcard view of the Lake in Walker Park, around 1900. Men, women and children would dress in their best clothes for a stroll in the park – here a group of people have stopped by the lake to admire the swans.

Left: The bandstand in Walker Park. The park was opened in 1891 and was one of a number of new parks in the North East at the time. The Victorians saw public parks as vital areas of clean air and recreation so local people could escape from crowded homes and the industrial work place.

Right: Lads pose in front of the Robert Burns Monument. The monument, provided by the Tyneside Burns Club in 1901, was removed in the 1970s and is now in council storage. In 2012 a £1.8 million Heritage Lottery Grant was awarded to redevelop Walker Park. One part of the plan is to restore the Burns Monument to the park.

Armstrong Park

The Monthly Chronicle of North Country Lore and Legend of 1888 featured this article on Armstrong Park.

It has been said by many who have had opportunities of judging, that the Armstrong Park at Newcastle, which now includes the famous Jesmond Dene, excels most other English public parks in picturesque beauty. It is situated, for the most part upon the eastern side of the valley of the Ouseburn. At one part it occupies both sides of the stream, extends from Heaton Hall on the south to Jesmond Towers on the north, and has an area of over one hundred acres. In traversing it you come upon every variety of scenery; steep wooded banks bordering over the burn and level bowling green and lawns. Shady walks under tall trees and open grass grown spaces, tangled thickets where the bracken grown in native wildness, and trim flower beds laid out with all the skills of the gardeners art; still ponds which reflect the overhanging foliage and rushing waterfalls which churn to foam the water of the little stream. Besides its natural and cultivated beauties, Armstrong Park has the attraction of historical associations to add to its interest.

The Cascade, Jesmond Dene.

The park is divided into three parts by roads which trisect it at right angles to its length. The southern portion (23 acres in area) was formerly part of the grounds of Heaton Hall. It was purchased by the Corporation of Newcastle, and opened to the public in 1879. On entering it by its south gate and standing on the plateau beside an ornamental temple like building, we have a magnificent view of Jesmond Dene. Seen in the evening, under a sun-set effect, it presents a charming picture, with the great masses of sombre foliage darkling under the glowing sky. Close by the south-east corner of the park is Heaton Hall, standing amongst tall trees. This picturesque old mansion, the residence of Colonel Addison Potter, stands on the site of a medieval building, remains of which still exists, and part of which is supposed to have been the chapel where, in 1299 King Edward I heard a boy bishop celebrate the vespers of St Nicholas. Heaton Hall received another royal visitor on the 1st May 1617, in the person of James I, who was then entertained by the owner, Henry Babington, and knighted his host here. The present building, erected by Matthew Ridley in 1713, is particularly interesting from its connection with the family now represented by Sir Matthew Ridley of Blagdon.

The old windmill in Armstrong Park.

Descending from the plateau, we reach the children's playground to which the legend 'keep off the grass' visible everywhere, does not apply. It is a rich boon to the people of the neighbourhood to have such a place set apart for the enjoyment of their little ones, and its advantages are appreciated and used to the utmost. Close at hand are the Bowling, Green and Croquet Ground, overlooked by a handsome terrace, and surrounded by beds of gorgeous flowers disposed in symmetrical designs, the whole hemmed in by the dark line of the tall forest trees. There are winding paths under these trees, deliciously cool in summer, and between their trunks we catch glimpses of the shining water of the burn. On the terrace is the aviary, generally well-tenanted by an interesting collection of birds, British and Foreign, and hard by is the fernery, where the monkey cage is a constant source of attraction to the children. Round at the back of the same building, a pair of gazelles also receive, at their daily levees, a fair share of visitors. In the north-east corner of this portion of the park, and close to the road which divides it from the next section, stands the ruin pile the community called 'King John's Palace'.

Lord Armstrong.

The second or middle portion of the park was a free gift of Sir William Armstrong (now Lord Armstrong) to the people of Newcastle. It was opened to the public on 23rd June 1880, and consists of 29 acres, lying, like the first portion, on the east bank of the burn. Our views of the old and of the rustic bridge will give some idea of its general appearance. The old tower was within living memory, a working windmill, and is of comparatively modern erection. It is a prominent and picturesque object from many points of view, and has been widely preserved on its lofty and breezy height.

On leaving the middle park by the north gate we find ourselves at the end of the iron bridge, usually called Benton Bridge, which here spans the Dene. It was built to the design of Sir William Armstrong, who also defrayed a great part of the cost of erection; is of light and elegant appearance, and of great convenience of those using Benton Bank. The view from it on either side is very fine. On the south we see the parks we have just left, with the old tower on the hill and the masses of foliage around it reflected in the Green Water Pool. Which lies far down below us in the valley. On the north we have a charming view of Jesmond Dene, which forms the third portion of the park, and, like the second, was the free gift of Lord Armstrong. The Jesmond Dene section of the park is now entered from the level of

Benton Bridge, by a new gate, as well as by the old doorway down in the valley, and from beginning to end it is a continual feast to the eye, fresh beauties appearing at every step.

The Bridge over Jesmond Dene.

Old Picture Postcards

We end with a few final old picture postcards of the area.

Playground, Heaton Park, N C on Tyne.   (158)

Children pose for the postcard photographer at the playground in Heaton Park. They occupy almost every piece of equipment and while some of the young 'uns look well dressed, there are others who are barefoot.

A rustic bridge in Heaton Park. This was originally a coloured postcard.

Christ Church, Walker with the Monument of Robert 'Honest Bob' Chambers on the left.

The "Aquitania" at Walker. 3447

Above: The *Aquitania* at Walker – another wonderful postcard by Johnston of Gateshead. The photograph was taken while the Cunard Line vessel was on the Tyne for refitting after the First World War.

160   BRIARWOOD CRESCENT. WALKERVILLE.

Right: Briarwood Crescent, Walkerville – the houses were built for the Model Cottage Exhibition of 1908.

SOUTH VIEW WEST
HEATON

Right: South View West, Heaton – a quiet view one hundred years ago.

A busy scene in Heaton Road in the early 1900s. A tram approaches from the distance, young lads stand in the road and a policeman, on the left, watches over everyone.

Also available from Summerhill Books

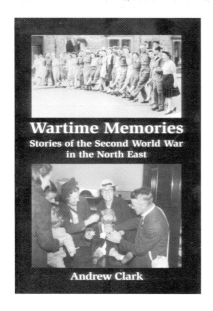